Moving to Britain from Poland

By Deborah Chancellor
Photography by Chris Fairclough

FRANKLIN WATTS
LONDON • SYDNEY

First published in 2008 by Franklin Watts

Franklin Watts,
338 Euston Road,
London, NW1 3BH

Franklin Watts Australia,
Level 17/207 Kent Street,
Sydney, NSW 2000

Series editor: Sarah Peutrill
Art director: Jonathan Hair
Design: Rita Storey
Photographs: Chris Fairclough (unless otherwise stated)

The Author and Publisher would like to thank the following for their
help in the preparation of this book: Karolina, Anna, Igor and the
staff and pupils at St Patrick's RC Primary School, Farnborough.

Picture credits: Ulrich Baumgarten/Vario images/Alamy: 12b.
bluliq/Shutterstock: 10t. Digital Food Shots/Shutterstock: 29b.
Family's personal photographs: cover (inset), 9b, 11b, 13b, 14b.
Jerzy/Shutterstock: 29t. Edyta Pawlowska/Shutterstock: 11t.
TauRanger/istock: 15t. Every attempt has been made to clear
copyright. Should there be any inadvertent omission please apply
to the publisher for rectification.

Dewey number: 304.8'41'0438

ISBN: 978 0 7496 7857 9

Printed in China

Franklin Watts is a division of Hachette Children's Books,
an Hachette Livre UK company.

Contents

Words in **bold** are in the glossary on page 28.

All about me

My name is Karolina. I am 11 years old and I like dancing, acting and writing stories. I have a pet rabbit called Fredek, who is very cute.

Fredek was a surprise Christmas present last year. His name is Polish for Frederick.

My family comes from Poland. We moved to Britain three years ago, when I was eight years old. Now we live in Farnborough, which is a town in the **county** of Hampshire in the south of England.

Meeting people
Try talking in Polish!

What is your name?
Jak się nazywasz?

My name is ...
Nazywam się

Look out for more Polish words in this book!

I like playing board games with my mum and dad. My favourite is Snakes and Ladders.

Meet my family

I get on well with my cousin Igor. He loves football, and plays for a local team.

I live with my mum and dad. I don't have any brothers or sisters, but my cousin Igor lives nearby. We sometimes meet after school.

Family words

Mum	*Mama*
Dad	*Tata*
Grandad	*Dziadek*
Grandma	*Babcia*

Most of my family still live in Poland. I keep in touch with them as much as I can. Although we live far apart, my grandparents are still very important to me.

I see my family when I go back to Poland. Here I am sitting with my grandad. They also come to visit me here in Britain.

I talk to my grandparents on the phone about twice a week.

About Poland

Poland is a country in Eastern **Europe**. It is smaller than some European countries, such as France and Spain, but it is bigger than Britain.

SWEDEN
FINLAND
NORWAY
ESTONIA **RUSSIA**
DENMARK **LATVIA**
LITHUANIA
KALININGRAD
UNITED KINGDOM
IRELAND **BELARUS**
NETHERLANDS **GERMANY** **POLAND**
BELGIUM
LUXEMBOURG **CZECH REP.** **UKRAINE**
FRANCE SLOVAKIA
LIECHTENSTEIN **AUSTRIA** **HUNGARY** **MOLDOVA**
SWITZERLAND
SLOVENIA CROATIA **ROMANIA**
MONACO BOSNIA AND SERBIA AND
HERZEGOVINA MONTENEGRO
ITALY **BULGARIA**
PORTUGAL ALBANIA MACEDONIA **TURKEY**
SPAIN **GREECE**

Poland

I can see where Poland is when I look at a map of Europe.

It takes just over two hours to fly from Poland to Britain.

There are lovely beaches in northern Poland. In central Poland, fields cover much of the land. In the south, near the **borders** with the Czech Republic and Slovakia, there are beautiful mountains.

Poland's highest mountain, Mount Rysy, is in the Tatra mountain range. It is 2,499m tall.

I went skiing in Poland when I was six years old, before we moved to Britain.

Karolina's mum says:

"When I was a child, I always went on holiday to the seaside in northern Poland. Now I take Karolina back there in the summer holidays."

My life in Poland

I was born in a city in southern Poland called Bytom (say 'Bittom'). My grandparents, uncles and aunts still live there. Bytom is a very old city. There used to be lots of **coal mines** in the area, but most of them are closed down now.

POLAND

•WARSAW

•Bytom

Bytom is quite a big city. It is a busy place.

My mum and I like looking at photos, to remind us of our life in Poland.

I liked living in Bytom. I had lots of friends there and the rest of my family lived near our home. We lived in a flat, which was nice and comfortable. It was bigger than the house we live in now in Farnborough.

Karolina's mum says:

"Karolina has always liked simple things. On her first birthday, her grandparents gave her an expensive toy elephant. She ignored it and played with a balloon instead!"

13

Moving to Britain

When I was eight years old, my mum got a new job in Britain. Mum's job was in Farnborough, so that is why we moved here. Dad came over later. It was really hard for me to leave my friends and family behind in Poland. We travelled to Britain by plane.

This is me on part of our journey to Britain. I brought one teddy with me, but no other toys.

LONDON

Farnborough

I was scared about coming to live in Britain. I didn't have any friends here, and I didn't know what to expect. Also, I couldn't speak any English.

We lived in a flat when we first arrived in Farnborough, but now we live in a house.

Karolina's mum says:

"When we moved to Britain, my biggest worry was that Karolina would not settle, and that we would have to move back to Poland again."

15

My new hometown

I like going shopping with my mum in Farnborough. Sometimes we go to a café for a treat.

My new **hometown** Farnborough is smaller and quieter than Bytom, where we used to live in Poland. About 57,000 people live in Farnborough. In Bytom, there are many more people – the city's **population** is about 200,000.

Lots of people who live in Farnborough have jobs in London, and travel to work every day by train. Some people work closer to home, like my mum. She helps to run a local **residential home**.

Mum has to leave home early to go to work, so my dad takes me into school in the morning.

Going to school

In Poland, I went to **kindergarten** before I started school. Like all Polish children, I didn't go to school until I was seven years old. I came to Britain when I was eight, and began at St Patrick's **Catholic** Primary School.

St. Patricks R.C. Primary School

Ruth and Kloe are two of my best friends. They are English. There are only three other Polish children at my school.

When I arrived at St Patrick's, I couldn't speak English. Three very nice teachers taught me to speak, read and write in English. They are my heroes, because they helped me so much.

Mrs Evans, Karolina's classroom assistant, says:

"Karolina tried to teach me Polish while I was teaching her English! She was confident from the start, and talked a lot, which helped her pick up English very quickly."

I don't need a special language teacher any more to help me at school. I can get on with work on my own now.

My school day

At my school in Poland, we had a different teacher for each subject, except maths and Polish, which were both taught by my class teacher. At St Patrick's, I only have one teacher, who stays with my class all day and teaches us all the subjects.

This is my teacher, Mrs Licence. My favourite subjects are history and maths, because I like learning and solving problems.

My school day begins at 8.50am, and ends at 3.30pm. There is a long lunch break in the middle of the day.

In Poland, most schools start at 8am, and finish early in the afternoon. Lessons are 45 minutes long, with a short break between each one.

Karolina's mum says:

"In Poland, Karolina was at the top of her class at school. When we moved to Britain, this changed, because she had to learn English. I think this was difficult for Karolina."

Keeping traditions

My family like to keep some Polish **traditions**. At Christmas we cook a special meal, which we eat on Christmas Eve. The meal has 12 courses. My favourite course is `**pierogi**`, which is a kind of pastry stuffed with tasty fillings.

I like cooking, especially at Christmas. I often help my mum in the kitchen.

Many Polish people celebrate their `name day`. There is a different Polish name for every day of the year. If your name is not on the **calendar** of traditional names, you can pick one of those names to celebrate as your `name day`.

Polish greetings

Happy Christmas!

Wesołych Świąt Bożego Narodzenia!

Happy name day!

Wszystkiego najlepszego z okazji imienin!

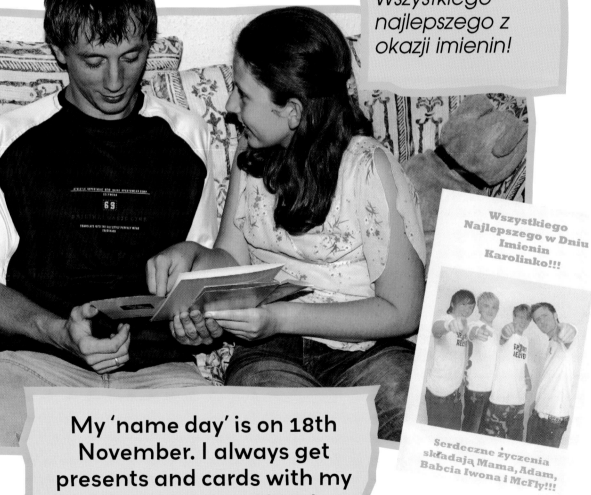

Wszystkiego Najlepszego w Dniu Imienin Karolinko!!!

Serdeczne życzenia składają Mama, Adam, Babcia Iwona i McFly!!!

My `name day` is on 18th November. I always get presents and cards with my name on them on this day.

My future

Next September I am going to start secondary school. My new school is in Farnham, a nearby town. I will have to get there by bus. I am a bit nervous, but also excited.

I always like to work hard, so I hope I will do well.

One day, I would like to go to **university**, but I don't know what I want to study yet.

When I grow up, I don't want to do the same thing as everyone else. I would like to do something to help people. I think I would like to join the Police one day.

I am happy living in Britain now, but I may move again one day. I have heard that Canada is a nice place!

Karolina's mum says:

"Karolina is a strong character, and could probably do most things. She will always want to learn more, and do more, in her life."

Glossary

borders
Lines, or boundaries, that separate two countries.

calendar
A list of all the dates of the year showing special events that occur on each day.

Catholic
Belonging to the Catholic faith. Roman Catholics are Christians that are led by the Pope in Rome.

coal mines
Places where coal is dug out of the ground.

county
One of the large areas that Britain is divided into.

Europe
One of the seven continents – large areas of land – of the world.

hometown
The town where you live.

kindergarten
A school or nursery for young children.

name day
A day when you celebrate your name, or a name chosen from the traditional calendar of Christian saints.

pierogi
A traditional Polish dish of stuffed pastry that is served at the Christmas Eve supper.

pollution
Dirty chemicals in the air and water.

population
The number of people who live in a place.

residential home
A place where people live who are unable to care for themselves.

traditions
Beliefs, customs or habits that have not changed for a very long time.

university
A place where some people go to study when they have left school.

Poland fact file

- More people live in Britain than in Poland. About 60 million people live in Britain, and about 40 million live in Poland.

- London, Britain's capital city, is 1,454 km away from Warsaw, the capital city of Poland.

Polish coins

- In Poland, people use a currency called the zloty. One hundred groszy make up one zloty – like in the British currency, which has one hundred pennies in a pound.

- Most people in Poland are Roman Catholics. Pope John Paul II, who died in 2005, came from Poland.

- Football is a very popular sport in Poland, just like it is in Britain.

- The Polish school year starts at the beginning of September, and ends in the middle of June. There are two school terms, called semesters, and a long summer holiday.

- When Polish children start school, they are given a large cone filled with sweets on this special day.

- In the past, Polish school children didn't have to wear school uniform, but this is changing. Many Polish school children now wear a uniform.

Polish flag

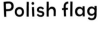

29

Index

Further information

www.polandonline.com
www.poland.dial.pipex.com
These websites give general information about Poland.

www.polishculture.co.uk
This website gives general information about Polish culture and traditions.

www.um.bytom.pl
This website gives information about Bytom, the Polish city where Karolina and her family used to live.

Note to parents and teachers: Please note that these websites are **not** specifically for children and we strongly advise that Internet access is supervised by a responsible adult.